# How to Become a God for Beginners

Roberto Benitez

Copyright © 2012 Roberto Benitez

All rights reserved.

ISBN: 0615613780
ISBN-13: 978-0615613789
ISBN: 1477419349
ISBN-13: 978-1477419342

# DEDICATION

This book is dedicated to Mariam, whose strength and wisdom encouraged me to finally finish my book.

# CONTENTS

|   | Introduction | i |
|---|---|---|
| 1 | Life Is A Dream | 3 |
| 2 | The Thought | Pg 18 |
| 3 | Staying In The Present Moment | Pg 24 |
| 4 | Hints And Tips | Pg 33 |

# INTRODUCTION

I've tried to make this book as short, and as simple, as possible. The reason being, this material is something everyone should know, and everyone should be able to utilize. Just like learning to walk or learning your ABC's, this material is something basic and fundamental. It shouldn't be difficult to understand or to master.

# 1 LIFE IS A DREAM

Life is a dream. That's it. That is the secret. You don't have to read the rest of this book. You are done, that is all you need to know.

If you are inclined to read further, start by understanding this, it is all happening inside your head. It is all in your mind. Everything you see in your life, everything you experience, is a dream that you have created.

Right now you are in that dream, just like when you are sleeping. The only difference between this, your waking dream, and the one when you are sleeping is time. Time works differently in this dream state than in your sleeping one. In your sleeping dream state everything moves at the speed of thought. In your waking dream (your normal life) everything moves at the speed of comprehension. In other words, things will happen as quickly or as slowly as what you really believe is possible. And, just like in a sleeping dream, you can manipulate this waking dream to make anything happen. **Anything**, just like a God.

<u>Lucid Dreaming</u>

You may be familiar with the term, lucid dream. . A **lucid dream**, in simplest terms, is a dream in which you are aware that you are dreaming. You can go on Amazon right now and look up books on lucid dreaming. In these books there are tips and strategies to manipulate your dreams. These strategies can be used to manipulate this waking dream state that you call your life.

## The Law of Attraction

If you are into metaphysics, then you have probably heard of "The Law of Attraction," as mentioned in the movie, "The Secret." The Law of Attraction states that "Like attracts like." In other words, your mind is constantly sending out thoughts into the universe, often in the form of wishes or desires, and they bounce back as your experience. What goes out comes back; what you think about you draw to you.

However, relying on the "Law of Attraction," at least in the conventional, sense is limited. I am not trying to discredit any other metaphysical books; everything they say is based in some truth, but what I am saying, is that there is a more fundamental reason why the Law of Attraction works, and it has little to do with positive thought waves, vibrations, signals or frequencies that you consciously project as others would have you believe. Everything that is happening in your world starts inside your mind yes, but specifically inside your subconscious mind; the same place that controls your dream state. Trust me; I have spent the last ten years trying to figure this all out, and through trial and error, I have reached a point where it now works for me 100% of the time. The key to understanding this is knowing that your subconscious mind creates everything, and how to make that work.

## Mind Verses Brain

Let's look more deeply. When I use the term *mind*, I am not talking about the brain. The brain is an organ, the mind is you. Your mind is divided into two parts: your conscious mind, which makes up about 3% of your total mind; and your subconscious mind, which makes up the other 97%. Right now, as you are reading this book, you are only using about 3% of your mind. The other 97% is off in the background creating your life. And, it is by far the larger and more powerful part of your mind. When you close your eyes and use your conscious mind to imagine yourself flying like Superman, the reason it does not happen, is because your subconscious mind says you cannot do it. The 3% would have to convince the 97%. Flying like Superman is not impossible, but you would need to use a much larger percentage of your mind in order to do it. I am going to show you how to accomplish this by using more of your subconscious mind to actively control the dream that is your life.

To start making this process work, you have to have a conscious thought of what you want and then bury it deep inside your subconscious mind like a seed. Here it will grow and eventually manifest in your life. As the thought takes hold in your subconscious mind, things in your life will begin to rearrange themselves to make the thought a present reality. Through this process you will literary have the power of a God at your fingertips. The power to create a dream that is to your liking.

The Catch

Sounds simple, doesn't it? So how come nobody is doing it? How come we all struggle so much to get what we want? Here is the catch, everybody *is* doing it. Including you. Everything that is happening in your life (the awake dream) is because of past, and now submerged thoughts, which are dominant in your subconscious. They are creating your reality. Everything. The weather, the war, TV shows, even *this* very book. You have participated in creating all of it through your subconscious mind. Your "dream" (the events in your life) shifted and changed to participate in that reality. Even the people that are in your life, including your children, are characters that you created in this dream; they are real, but not as real as you think they are.

The reason why most people are not having more success at getting what they think they want, is because they come at it with their conscious minds. They are focused on consciously controlling things; trying to make things happen with the 3% of their mind, while the 97% is really running the show. Instead of imagining yourself having a better job, you look for a better job. Instead of seeing yourself having more money, you work overtime to get more money. You are working with your current dream or illusion (your job) to create another illusion (more money); why not just change the illusion?

The subconscious mind is what creates reality and to change your current reality you need to change your subconscious thoughts. Do not misunderstand me; there is nothing wrong with using your **conscious** mind to make your life better by working within your current dream. But it is important to know you have another options. You can live your life without using metaphysics; we do it all the time, but if you are not getting the results you want, it is worth learning how to better control your conscious dream.

There is a serious downside to making things happen from the conscious mind, it can be a lot of work.

For example, you want a good job. So you go to school for four years and graduate only to find out there is no job market out there. You then go back to school for an extra two years to get an advanced degree. Trying to get results from a conscious place can produce results, but it also can really wear you down. There is an easier way.

## The Skill: Disciplining Your Thoughts

The most important skill you can learn if you want to master this process, is disciplining your mind; a skill most people never learn. The reason it is so important, is because your thoughts are going to manifest in some way at some time, no matter what. So, wouldn't you rather choose thoughts that create good things? Yet, we think all kinds of random and negative thoughts about things we don't want to happen. The reason why random stuff happens, is because you have filled your mind (conscious and subconscious) with random thoughts. The reason negative things happen in your life, is because you have worried or obsessed about things you don't want to happen, and those negative thoughts manifest.

Throughout much of every day our thoughts are random. For example, when you are driving in your car your mind is often wandering, and those random thoughts can come from anywhere. They can be something you talked about at work, something you heard on the radio, something you saw on a billboard or bumper sticker. You may spend that time worrying about your bills, or your health, or your children. Those negative thoughts are also little directives that actually increase the chance of bad things happening.

You probably wouldn't choose any of those

thoughts, if you knew they were going to take form in your life. But, all those thoughts can and do slip into your subconscious, and contribute to your reality. Whether good thoughts or bad thoughts, they are going to become part of your conscious dream in some way.

How big a part of your life they become depends on how big a space they take up in your subconscious, and what other thoughts are already there that support them or contradict them. It is very important to discipline your thinking to be in alignment with the things you want.

Moving Thoughts from Conscious to Subconscious

If you want to create something specific in your life, think about what you want, and then bury those thoughts into your subconscious mind. From there they will manifest. The two most important things connected to burying a thought, are the level of **emotion/intensity,** and the amount of **repetition**. If you have a thought that has a lot of emotion connected to it, either positive or negative, it will be heavier and sink easier down into your subconscious mind. In contrast a thought that doesn't have much feeling attached to it, won't hold much weight in your subconscious. Thoughts that you have over and over again, will also eventually sink down into your subconscious mind.

Being aware of what you think about, especially those thoughts that you think over and over in repetition every day, or those thoughts that get you really upset, or make you really happy, is an important first step in understanding what is going into your subconscious for manifestation. You have to be aware of what you think before you can make a conscious choice to change your thoughts.

Your life, and what you have in it, is a result of both disciplined and undisciplined thoughts you have had in the past. If you want to change your conscious dream, you must become aware of what you think, and the emotion attached to it. This is what you are feeding into your subconscious.

## The Trap of Overthinking

Some people believe if they just think about something over, and over, and over, it will manifest. This is true, and not true. If you can think about something with great confidence, it is okay to think about it over, and over, and over. However, most people can't do that. When you think about something repeatedly, you usually begin to worry that the good thing isn't going to happen, or a bad thing is going to happen. You won't get the job, or you will get cancer. Overthinking becomes a trap, because it often turns to the negative and that is not what you want to manifest. You think about wanting a new job and more money, but then worry you won't get it. What goes into your subconscious as the stronger thought is what has the most emotion attached to it, and that can often be the negative, which is what you will create.

When you hold tight to a thought, and worry about an outcome, your conscious mind can also act as a doorway, not letting thoughts sink into your subconscious. Anytime you focus too much on a thought, that thought will remain on the surface in your conscious mind and not sink down into your subconscious. This might sound like a contradiction because we need to focus on our thoughts repeatedly, but not too repeatedly. We need to hold a thought about what want as long as we can stay consistently focused on that particular thought, and not let it become something else.

There is a balance to thinking about what you want, before releasing it to sink into your subconscious. If you don't think about it enough, it won't be a dominant enough thought to manifest. But on the other hand, thinking too much can trap you as well. You must work with your thinking on many levels and find a balance that works. I recommend having a strong thought about something you want, and then letting it go. I will describe this further as the book progresses.

## Letting Go

Many spiritual traditions talk about the importance of letting go. If you try to control the outcome of what you want, you are using your conscious mind to do it, and that is not how to manifest.

The hardest thing about metaphysics is learning to give up your conscious control of everything. That means you don't figure out how to make something happen, you only focus on the end result, not how to get there. You cannot try to control the outcome of your goal. You have to conceptualize it, think about it, and then let it go and let your goal come to you.

For example, if you don't have a car, and you want a car, you have to see yourself driving and owning a car. Focus on the end result; see yourself driving the car, smell the car, feel your hands on the steering wheel. Then let it go and it will sink deep into your subconscious. After that, just focus on something else entirely, don't try to find a way to get the money to buy that car.

In the metaphysical world, we approach things by letting the Universe (your subconscious mind) create the outcome, because the universe knows better. You could try from your conscious mind to find a way to get the car. You could get a second job, or borrow the money from someone. But that is not how The Law of Attraction works, and you are wasting energy. You will easily attract what you want, and need, in your life, if you acknowledge the desire and then let it go. It needs to sink down into your subconscious, so the Universe can create it. If you follow this process, a car will come to you.

When you start consciously using this process, it can be very hard to let go of the doing. We are trained in this society that doing is best, so at first you're going to feel useless. By this I mean ineffectual, because we believe in our conscious minds we need to do something to make things happen. But, you may as well give yourself permission to feel like a bum, because you cannot be successful if you interfere with the process.

If you follow these instructions, about 90% of the time you will achieve your goal in an unexpected way. In this example you will end up with a car. A car that is better suited to you, or more affordable, or just better in general, than if you went out and made it happen. Maybe you'll get it from a friend or a family member. Perhaps you'll win it in a raffle or some unexpected contest; you never know.

What you don't want to do is worry, or think too much, or look for ways to make it happen. The thoughts you attach to the car (good or bad), will eventually sink down into your subconscious mind. If you worry, the desire for the car will have a negative outcome attached to it, the opposite of what you want.

It is best to think about what you want, like the car, either with complete confidence or only briefly when it pops into your head. Don't make a conscious effort to think about it too much. If it does pop into your head, just acknowledge it, "There's that car again. I really do want it, and I am going to get it!" Then let it go, as best you can. Let it go and think about something else entirely. Let it go and let the Universe do the work of manifesting it.

In the beginning it's going to be on your mind all the time, and you will have to work to let it go. After a while you're not going to dwell on it as much and you will just think about it occasionally. When I started writing this book, I was going to suggest a routine of visualizing your goals in the morning and at night. But then I changed my mind. It's a really tricky subject. If you're very disciplined about staying positive, and confident, about what you want, then by all means do the visualizing morning and night. Picture what you want and then let it go. But, if you have a hard time controlling your mind, and the thought does come up at unplanned times, just KNOW in the moment you're going to get it. Briefly picture having it and tell yourself, "That was a preview of what is to come." Then move on, let it go.

For example, think about how you would feel if you knew you were getting a certain toy for Xmas. Your parents have locked it in the closet but you know it's coming, so you start daydreaming of playing with it. You just can't wait!

That's the state of mind you want to have! Total confidence that it is coming.

To put this concept of letting go in an even simpler way, imagine you are inside your car and you're waiting for the light to change. You're wanting the light to turn green, which is your present thought. After a while you start getting irritated and tired of waiting, so you decide to text or call someone. As soon as you start texting or dialing the number, the light turns green!

Trust me that was no coincidence. The reason the light turns green at that moment is because you focused 100% of your attention on your cell phone. You let go, and the thought of the green light was no longer being held on the surface in your conscious mind. It had a chance to sink undisturbed into your subconscious to manifest.

The fact that you were upset about the traffic light gave it some added strong emotion for it to sink down quickly. You can try this when you are driving, but don't just *pretend* to use you cell phone, really do it. Your mind will know the difference. You actually have to call somebody you want to talk to, and it will work.

Focus on the Present

The most effective way to focus elsewhere after you have your goal thought, is to **immediately focus on something in the present moment**. The present is your best friend. When you focus in the present, your mind is in neutral, there are no thoughts running through your head to interfere with your goal thought. You are just observing what is going on in front of you. So, rather than trying to control your thoughts in order to keep them positive and confident, you can just focus on the **present moment**; your brain will do the rest. Later on I will discuss some tips on how to do this with more ease.

Hard Work

Staying in the present requires the ability to discipline your mind. One thing that helps is the understanding that hard work has no value. It is meant to drain your will. The harder you work, the more exhausted you will become, and the more difficult it will be to discipline your mind. "Hard work builds character," yeah right! Hard work destroys character! Hard work makes people dull; it turns them into zombies. A better term would be, "Discipline builds character." Human beings were not designed to work hard, they were designed to manifest through their subconscious minds. That is how we have the power of God at our fingertips.

Addicted to Thinking

In our society we have been taught to think backwards. We are indoctrinated from childhood to think a certain way. We go to school where we learn to problem solve, so we can then make a living. This is not necessarily a bad thing per se, but problem solving is not the only way to think that can earn you a living.

In a metaphysical reality, we would use our brains 10% of the time for problem solving, and 90% of the time for having fun and being in the present moment. Instead we are taught to use about 40% of our brain to solve problems and the other 60% to think and worry about the problem's outcome. This process creates an addiction to thinking; you go round, and round, and round in your thoughts. Plus, anytime you are thinking about something over and over, and trying to solve it, you are thinking about ways it can't or won't happen, you are filling your mind with negative options. If you are always worried, guess what, all that worrying, all those negative thoughts will sink into your subconscious mind. So eventually, all your worries are going to manifest into reality. What you repeat in your mind over and over, you come to believe at a very deep level.

Thinking all the time is an addiction, it is a disease that plagues the human race. Eckhart Tolle, in his famous book "The Power of Now," suggests just that. According to Tolle, thinking all the time feels normal, because it is the way we all are taught to operate. But, it's not normal. He believes we do it because it is an easy escape from our terrible present reality, almost like a drug. You look out at the world, our world of war and poverty, disease and destruction, and you just want to escape, so you think about your life, you plan for the future, you worry about how to make things better, or you escape completely and think about a fantasy life, sex, or fun things you can do in the future, you problem solve and plan.

But look at a two-year-old. That child is walking around observing everything, maybe looking for something to play with. He or she is not worried about where their food is going to come from, or who is going to change their diapers. That child is permanently in the present, and not thinking about the future or the past. Thinking in the present moment is normal; we are born normal.

It is around the age of six that we start losing our focus on the present moment. With lots of support from problem solving adults, who ask children to think about what you will wear to school tomorrow, what we will do on the weekend, and what you want to be when you grow up, we learn to think out of present time. At around age six we become self-aware and develop the capacity to project into the future or the past. According to Eckhart Tolle that's a good skill to have if you need to problem solve, or you need to anticipate the future, or learn from experiences in the past, but as time goes by this type of thinking becomes very addictive, and that creates the problem. We become unhappy with our present situation, so our minds go somewhere else.

I dare you to go through the entire day without thinking about something that happened in the past or contemplating something that might happen in the future. This includes thinking about something that happened thirty seconds ago or something that's going to happen ten minutes from now. I guarantee you won't even last fifteen seconds without thinking about something outside of the present moment.

Summary

To summarize what I have said so far, you are always manifesting things in your life (dream) like a god; you really don't have to read this book to learn that. You are already born with that ability. It's automatically on all the time, whether or not you believe it. You can never turn it off, and you can't turn it on, because it is always on. You are doing it 24 hours a day. However, the things that are happening in your life can appear random and out of your control, because your thoughts are generally random and are not being controlled. For the most part, we are addicted to this kind of undisciplined thought. Everybody seems to have ADD (attention deficit disorder) for lack of a better term.

The only discipline that we are taught by our parents and teachers, is to organize all the resources we have in this dream (money, brains, good looks, connections etc.) and make a better life by putting these resources together in the best possible way. Instead I'm going to teach you how to discipline your mind, so that you can control your dream. If you were born into poverty, guess what! You don't need stay there. You can change your dream and create any lifestyle you want. You don't have to work your but off, or go back to school to make a living. You can just skip all that, and be rich. Or choose not to be rich; just create everything you want by manifesting it directly without money. In order to create exactly what you want in this life (dream) 100% of the time, you have to have a disciplined mind.

With that disciplined mind, you would have a thought about what you want, hold it briefly in your mind (positively and with repetition), feel intense emotion attached to it, and then let it go, **immediately** focusing on something else. This is done like a wish or a prayer. You think the thought, "I really, really want a new job." You think it with emotion, anticipating a wonderful new job, and you think about it for a minute or two. Then you let it go. Don't overthink it, just let it sink into your subconscious where the Universe will take over and make it happen. You may need to experiment with how much time you spend thinking about it, how much is enough and how much is too much, before letting it go, but this process will work.

# 2 THE THOUGHT

A thought is a thought, no matter what. You can have a very long thought, or a very short thought, a very complicated thought, or a very simple thought. For the most part, it doesn't matter. Don't waste time trying to make your thoughts perfect, just be aware that your thoughts are what is creating your reality; that is a fact. All your thoughts combined make up your life (dream), both your good thoughts and your bad thoughts will become a part of your reality.

## Through Your Own Eyes

Since you know that your thoughts are going to manifest in some way, at some time, be aware of what you are thinking and focus on things you want. For example, if you don't have a car and you want a car, think about owning a car, and imagine yourself driving that car. Imagine yourself driving it right, now not in the future. You don't have to specify what kind of car it is, just think about driving it down the highway and that will be enough. Just being generally aware of what you want is sufficient to manifest it.

If on the other hand you want to be specific, that is fine too. Picture exactly the make and model of the car you would like. Picture the color, the interior, the feel of the seats. Whichever way you prefer, general or specific, it doesn't matter.

What does matter is that you need to think about the car in a certain way if you want it to happen. Don't see yourself inside a car from a distance, like in a picture or a movie, literally experience yourself inside the car. You must be inside the experience, see your hands on the wheel, feel the seats, and be looking out the windshield. Experience yourself inside the car; driving it in present time. This process works better if you see what you want through **your own eyes.**

You should be able to see your hands, your feet, the steering wheel, but you cannot see your own face. When you think of yourself inside the car try to include all five senses in your image. What does that car smell like, what does it feel like, what does it sound like. That's how you have to see images to make them happen. The only time you would be able to see your face is if you looked in the rearview mirror, other than that **always imagine whatever you want through your own eyes**, not as if you were watching a movie, but as if you were inside the movie. This is very important!

## Holding a Thought

Also don't concern yourself with how long your thought lasts. It doesn't matter, what matters is that the thought stays **consistent.** Keep the thought as long as you can hold it .If you have a thought you want to manifest, don't let it morph into something else. Think the thought for as long as you can before it changes into something else.

Eventually you will get to the point where you can keep a thought in your head for minutes at a time. If you have a hard time holding the image steady, then tell yourself out loud what the image contains. "This car smells like new leather, it feels warm, and the seats hold me just right. It sounds like a purr when I drive it. I like having the window down so I can feel the wind." Make the image vivid as you experience it.

Here's a simple exercise to increase your ability to hold a thought and it works wonders. Sit down in a comfortable chair and focus on an object somewhere in the room. It doesn't matter what it is or where it is; pick anything, a book, a vase, a cup, a pencil. Try to focus only on that object for least five minutes, without any other thoughts coming into your head. Do this every day.

At first it may be fairly difficult, but after the first couple of days it will get much easier. Eventually, you will be able to focus on a thought for minutes without it changing into something else. This is how you learn to discipline your mind.

Emotion

The more emotional you are about a thought, either positive or negative, the heavier the thought is going to be and the easier it will sink down into your subconscious. The more emotion you attach to the image the faster it is going to manifest.

Emotion is easier for some people than others. If you are a woman, you are likely emotional by nature. So for a woman to put emotion into an image/thought is not difficult, in fact it's second nature. For a man it is different, and I will tell you why. Anytime a man has an orgasm, he becomes emotionless for at least four days. After four days without an orgasm, a man becomes restless and emotional, full of energy and drive. That is one of the reasons why all monks and yogis from India practice celibacy. As a man, you can practice celibacy to become more emotional and bring about your thoughts/desires faster than any other way on this planet. However, if you don't want to do this, then by all means skip it, it is not necessary. But trust me, for men, it will make the process a hell of a lot faster if celibacy is practiced until you achieve your goal.

<u>Working a Thought</u>

As I have mentioned previously repetition can be one way to bury a thought into your subconscious mind. You want to repeat the thought/image with confidence that it is happening, but again not too many times, because that can keep the thought on the surface. You have to find a balance of making the thought a strong and dominant thought, but not an obsessive thought.

While you are focusing on a thought it is on the surface, in your conscious mind. You only want it to stay there for a short while, so attach strong emotion to it, get a clear picture of it, and feel confident about it, then surrender it to your subconscious. You hand it over to your subconscious by letting it go, so it can slip away from your conscious and sink down. The Universe (subconscious mind) will take care of the rest.

If you are a beginner, I suggest you focus on what you want just once a week. As you become more disciplined about staying in the present, you can then work your way up to once in the morning right after you wake up, and once at night before you go to bed, every day. In between those times, you want to be focused on the present, and nothing else. Think it and forget it. Don't dwell on the thought, don't dwell on anything. Keep moving forward; stay in the present moment. If you think you made a mistake, or did it wrong, forget about it. Keep moving forward, stay in the present.

Right before you go to bed is the best time to focus on your thought, because once you go to sleep you are not thinking about anything. You're just asleep. So the thought can just sink down into your subconscious without any interference.

## Starting Small

Another thing about this process is t that it is easier and faster to manifest little things than big things. You can manifest a $20 bill, a phone call from an old friend, or a lost book quite quickly and easily. But bigger things, like a lottery check, a new car, or a relationship are more difficult. They are going to take longer, because you don't have as much confidence about your ability to manifest them. Also those thoughts are newer to your subconscious.

If you have experience with winning a lottery, then that image is already in your subconscious mind, and it is easier to believe it, and easier to create it again. The reason you can manifest little things so easily, is because they've been part of your life for so long and they already have a permanent space in your subconscious mind.

## Summary

In this section about The Thought, I explained how thoughts need to be handled. First, you always need to see things **through you own eyes** as though you are having the experience you wish for **right now**, not like you are viewing a movie, or seeing it in the future, but as if you are actually in the movie at this moment and looking around.

Next you need to discipline your thinking so you can hold a thought **consistent** and not let it change randomly. The important thing is not how long you hold it, but that you hold it for as long as you can; keeping it the same.

You need to experience the thought **with emotion**. If you feel nothing about the thought, your subconscious can hardly register it. You have to repeat it many, many, many times to have the same impact as if you just feel very strongly about it.

You must work all of these things together when trying to manifest a thought. See it through your own eyes, keep it consistent, and attach emotion to it. All the things you now have in your life have come from this process even though you were not aware of it. When you want to be a God and manifest things that you choose, you have to start small, and build up confidence and familiarity in your subconscious. You can actually start by working this thought process on small things and watch them happen!

# 3 STAYING IN THE PRESENT MOMENT

As I said before, the present moment is your best friend, and especially when it comes to manifesting. The first ten seconds after you have a thought are extremely important. As soon as you are done with your thought, immediately start focusing on your present situation; whatever is at hand. Focus on the trees, on your shoes, your hands, the cars driving by. It takes a while for the chemicals in your brain to do their job. Remember at least ten seconds! However, the longer you can stay in the present the better.

Your brain specifically goes to work during the resting phase, not the action phase. You think a thought and let it go by focusing on the present, and then the subconscious can go to work manifesting it. When you lift weights and exercise you do not build muscle. Your body builds muscle after a workout, when it is resting. This is when it gets stronger. The same is true for sleep, the body builds and repairs when it is at rest.

A similar thing is true for your brain. If you are studying for a test and you start to get tired, you have reached the point of diminishing returns, the point where you can no longer take in information. If you take a break, then all that information will seep into your brain.

To further this example, imagine that your brain is an empty glass. When you study the glass starts getting filled with water (information). As soon as you take a break or go to sleep, that is when you start drinking from the glass and your body takes in the information. If you're studying while tired the glass can overflow with water and spill on the floor.

No matter how much more you study the information is not going to get into your brain unless you take a break to let the previous information sink in. This goes for any activity involving your brain, whether it memorizing a grocery list, playing the piano, or learning some new task. The information becomes more permanent when you take a break to let it sink in.

In order to do this with your thoughts you need to think them, and then release them, and focus in the present moment. I think the hardest part of this whole process is learning how to let go and stay in the present.

<u>If a Tree Falls</u>

It helps if you realize that the most important thing happening on this planet, is what you are looking at this very moment. Many metaphysical authors tell us that the present moment is really all there is. The government does not exist, your job does not exist, your parents do not exist. Unless you put your attention on them, and actually see them right in front of you, they do not exist. Your job will exist tomorrow when you go to work, but it does not exist right now. Even quantum physics is coming to this conclusion, as soon as you take your attention away from something, it ceases to exist.

Philosophers have argued for ages the question of, "If a tree falls in the forest and nobody hears it, does it make a sound?" and the answer is "NO," not unless you are there to hear it. In fact, not only does it not make a sound, it doesn't exist at all, unless you are there and experiencing it/creating it. It may not seem like a big deal, but trust me it is. It is all the difference in the world. Remember, this is only a dream. **Your** dream. **Nothing exists unless you put your full attention on it. That is how we create and how we experience.**

If you are depressed thinking about things in the future, like going to work tomorrow, it is a total waste of time! It is just a possible scenario in the back of your mind; it has not happened yet, and there is no guarantee that it is going to happen. The only thing that is guaranteed, is what is happening right now. That is what you have created so far, what you have to experience, and the only thing that is real. What is going on in the present moment is the only thing that can harm you. If you are worried about what can happen tomorrow, don't. If it is in the future is has no bearing on now. It cannot touch you, and you have the power to change it before it happens.

<u>Fun</u>

The easiest way to stay in the present, is to have fun! When you play video games, time flies by. When you are out at a club dancing you lose track of time, when you are watching your favorite television show, bam, it is already over. Fun is the easiest way to stay in the present moment.

Also while you are having fun, all your thoughts manifest themselves more quickly because they are not being disturbed. They are being allowed to sink into the subconscious mind without interruption. Another way to have fun, is to work on perfecting your craft. Whatever it is, focus on doing it the best way possible. If you are at your job, try to focus on every little detail and immerse yourself in the doing of it, enjoy it and have fun.

## Moving Forward

Another important skill to master is the ability to keep moving forward. Anytime you are done with a task, move on to the next one. Do not hesitate, do not dwell on it, and do not give it a second thought. That second thought will kill you. You already finished the task so stop thinking about it. Whether you did it perfectly or poorly doesn't matter. It is done; keep moving.

I don't mean to sound cliché but "It is not how many times you fall, it is how quickly you get up again." Keep moving…You have to be like a robot, move on to the next challenge and focus on it 100%.

## Illusions

Do not get sucked into any of your illusions. We tend to put too much focus on our job, career, people in our lives, and they are all just illusions in this dream. They are holograms if you will and not real. Do not pay any attention to them unless they are right in front of you. Do not let any authority figures like your parents, school, politicians, the police, or your boss fool you. You are the authority. You are God. Believing otherwise is giving your power to an illusion. They behave the way you want them to behave based on your past perceptions and thoughts. If you don't like it, then change the image in your head, and let it go; move on. You change the illusion by changing your thoughts.

## Feeling Like a Bum

If, after you start getting into the habit of letting go, you start feeling like a "bum," that means you are doing it right! Letting go of always taking action, letting go of trying to control the outcome, and letting go of your worries, makes you feel irresponsible, "like a bum," but you are not! Feeling like an irresponsible bum means you are moving in the right direction. I am not saying don't take care of business, what I am saying is, once you take care of business don't dwell on it, don't redo it, don't stay focused on it. Move on to the next thing; move on to the next responsibility that you have. If you think something negative is going to happen, replace it with an image of a good outcome, and then focus on what is presently in front of you. Letting go can really make you feel like a bum, but that is perfectly okay.

## Focus on the Rope

It might seem silly to be focusing on the leaves on the trees, the dirt on the ground, the keyboard on your desk, or the socks on your feet, but this can help you stay in present time. Think about it, children do it all the time. To them it is normal. It **is** normal. We are born normal.

As I said earlier, we start to think differently around the age of six. Before that, children are only looking for something to play with; they engage with whatever is in front of them. Their desires for food, shelter, and warmth are subtle thoughts at the back of their minds, and because they are only focused on the present moment, these subtle thoughts will be fulfilled. Your subtle thoughts will manifest too. If you are hungry, you don't have to create an image of a pizza in your mind, as long as you stay focused on your present task, just the subtle thought of food is enough to manifest the perfect food showing up to satisfy your hunger.

Imagine you are floating on a raft with no sail, and the only way to get to land is to shoot an arrow with a rope attached to it all the way to the shore. When it reaches land, it will anchor deep in the sand. The beach is your goal, your image. All you have to concern yourself with is pulling on that rope. All your focus and all your attention should be on pulling the rope which is the present time activity, you don't even have to look at the beach anymore, staying in present time will get you there. Just focus on pulling on that rope, eventually you will reach your goal and pull yourself to land.

<u>Leap of Faith</u>

You live in this box called the present; this is your dream. All of the resources you have created to fulfill your dreams and be happy, are only available inside this box. Your job, your bank account, and your friends, are all the things you have created so far, and they make up the box. Try to focus on appreciating these resources and utilizing them in a way that makes your life better. If you are missing resources from your box, then use your thinking to create what you need. Hold an image of the desired resource in your mind and then quickly turn your focus back inside the box. You only have to hold the image in your head for a few seconds, or a few minutes if you can, it does not really matter as long as you can hold the image steady in your head.

Letting go and letting the thought/image sink down into your subconscious mind is the hardest part. If you want to talk about "leaps of faith," that is the biggest Leap; asking for something in your mind, completely letting go of any worry or concern, and trusting it will come. Just take the leap and only focus on what is taking place right in front of you.

## Receiving

Knowing how to receive is also important. Receiving is a condition where you do not try to make your wish happen, you understand it will happen on its own. Receiving is a state of mind where you believe good things will come to you, but you don't effort on their behalf. If you try to imagine how your wish is going to be fulfilled, you are just slowing it down. Again, your job is to have the thought and then stay in the present. Trying to make your wish happen by pushing it along is not part of this book. Do not look for the ways it is going to come. Also, don't wait in anticipation of it either, just focus on things in the present. If you are waiting for your desire to arrive, then that state of waiting will become your present reality. When you experience the thought in your mind, enjoy it as if it is already yours, but that is it. Do not dwell on it, this puts you in a place to receive it.

## Summary

All you have to do is have a thought, and then forget about it by staying in the present; after that your wish\desire will come to you. That's it. This whole book can be summed up in that one statement. The rest is just details. Your subconscious mind is the ultimate form of leverage. Don't let your conscious mind try to solve the problem.

The hardest part is staying in the present. The only work you need to do is to have the thought. Your conscious mind is only going to be used to plan stuff, not to make stuff. Remember that!

This whole process is very similar to how the power of prayer works also. If you pray over and over again to God for a certain outcome, you are sinking repeated thoughts into your unconscious. People tend to pray for things that are important and meaningful, and that they have strong emotion about. If your faith is strong, you let it go and "leave it in the hands of God." Consequently, you don't interfere with the process, you focus on your life after making the prayer and it usually gets taken care of in the end.

I say *usually* because prayer doesn't always work. What sometimes happens is we start to lose faith, and then we tell ourselves "God doesn't exist," and we try to find a solution ourselves which is not staying in the present, this is when the conscious mind takes over, and interferes with the desired outcome. Staying in the present, after you ask for what you want, is what makes the process work.

Try this. Imagine your mind is a river, the current represents your running thoughts. Your goal is to place rocks (specific thoughts) at the bottom of the river, one on top of the other until they build up and eventually reach the surface. When the rocks (thoughts) reach the surface, they manifest. The current however can knock them over.

There are two ways to help get the rocks stacked up so they reach the surface. First, is to drop down bigger rocks. Second, is to stop the current. To drop bigger rocks, your thoughts have to be filled with vivid images and strong emotion. To stop the current, you have to stop having random thoughts, you have to discipline your thinking and stay in the present moment. If you do both of these things, you can build up the rocks in relation to any given desire, so that they will manifest rather quickly.

Because it is cumulative, as long as you keep dropping down the same thoughts over, and over, and over again, eventually they will reach the surface and manifest.

If you stop building up the rocks (focused thought) for say a month, the current will take away the rocks (thoughts). **Your brain is the muscle that keeps reality together.** If you stop repeating specific thoughts and let your mind wander, after a while your brain will begin to atrophy, your thought focus will dissipate, and you will lose all the work that you have accomplished. Just like any other muscle.

# 4 HINTS AND TIPS

Everything is your property. Everything you see belongs to you. The trees, the houses, the streets, the buildings, the Earth, the sky, the people. All of these things are under your control. There is nothing that is out of your control. Things are like little plastic soldiers that you have collected and can place wherever you want them, and how you want them. You set up the pieces, and make them move just like a game of chess. Again, it's your dream.

You have to think of the present as your playground. You have to have fun with it. Always remember that all the bad things that happen can be undone. Never take anything too seriously. If you make a mistake, whether consciously or unconsciously, just go back and fix it. There is no need to rush; there is no need to panic. Have fun with it.

Don't talk about what you want with anybody; talking about it lessens the emotion. Keep what you want inside your head. There is a big debate as to whether or not you should say things out loud or keep them in your mind. It has been my experience that keeping what you want inside works faster, NEVER say it out loud. Just keep repeating it inside your head.

It is easier to move on when you do not procrastinate. Do not dwell on the past or the future. If something bad happens, just work on fixing it. You have to keep moving, you cannot stop. The only time you should ever stop, is when you reach your goal. At that point, you want to savor the moment, but again don't stay too long in that one place. Move on to your next objective. You don't have to wait for something important to happen to start your life!

One easy way to stay in the present is to spend time in nature; go for a hike in the woods, or walk on the beach. Whenever you are in nature, things are constantly transforming. The trees are always growing and their leaves are always changing. So, as you walk in nature things are never the same. Nature keeps you in the present, there is always something new to see. As opposed to being in the city, where the buildings and the streets never change. When you walk or drive in the city, your mind wanders. The concrete and cement are always the same so your mind is easily bored.

You are on your own. Always remember that all responsibility lies with you. Do not count on anybody else to help you, and do not blame anyone else either. You are the source of everything that happens to you, not anyone else, and only you can get yourself out of it. If something bad happens, immediately start thinking something positive to counter it, then go back to the present. Do not get upset with anyone else, it is all up to you. You need to take back control of your circumstances, don't let the circumstances control you.

Take pride in what you create, you can use it to build a better life. Do not be ashamed of what you create, whether good or bad. Again, always remember that it can be undone. In church, they teach you to love your enemy. The reason is, you created your enemy. You created the terrorists. You created the war. If you start hating your enemy, then what you are actually doing, is hating what you have created. This puts more emotion on the creation and makes it harder to get rid of. If you love your enemy, and realize he or she is just one of your creations, you can change that creation.

Your life (dream) is a twenty-four hour mission; you always have to be on it. Remember you are God, and you cannot turn it off. Whether or not you believe it, it is true, so it helps to be mindful of what is going on in your head. If you slip up and find yourself thinking something negative, just stop and choose positive thoughts. In the beginning it may seem like too much work. Don't take it too seriously. If you make a mistake, just go back to the positive. It does not have to be perfect, eventually it will become second nature, so go at your own pace.

Your only concern should be what is in your field of view. Those are the only things that are important. Your present reality is all that matters. Again, the past and the future are illusions; the only real thing is the present moment. If you keep focusing on the present, everything will fall into place when the time is right. You only get to entertain yourself with what is right in front of you. Focus on perfecting your craft, which is staying in the present.

This may all seem imaginary, but it is real. At first your goals are going to seem impossible, like they are never going to happen. You have to remember that they will happen if you let them. Do not force them, focus on what you want, then let it go, and it will come to you. **Let your subconscious mind do all the work, your only job is to tell your subconscious mind what you want.** Don't try to directly control it, just live it. If something bad happens, experience it; go through the process. Do not fight it. After the unwanted experience is over, replace it with the desire for a better outcome.

You are the one that is building this world, not the government, not the Church, not the schools, only you. As I have said before, **You** are the creator. Take credit for everything that happens.

Your life is a dream that you are building. It is not as real as you think, so do not get overly attached to it. The Tibetan monks practice lack of attachment with their sand painting. They create beautiful pieces of art using millions of grains of colored sand. When they are done, they sweep it away, and it becomes nothing. They have no attachment. They are practicing non-attachment.

The world can wait until you finish what you're doing right now. Do not feel like you have to rush to keep appointments or schedules. The world is moving at the pace you create, which means you can slow it down if you want to. Disciplining your mind by knowing what you want and then focusing on the present is more important than anything else that is going on in your life. Because the world is under your control, it can wait until you complete what you are doing in the present moment.

Your brain is a muscle that is very malleable. Just like your body, it is not in a permanent state. When your subconscious mind accustomed becomes accustomed to a thought, it will stay there until you replace it. And, just like your body; if you don't keep exercising it, it will revert back to its previous state. Your brain is the most powerful, most useful organ you have; make sure you take care of it with discipline and healthy thoughts.

DO NOT write down your plans/goals on paper. All the other metaphysics books will tell you to do this step, but skip it! If you write it down it is already expressed in your dream and it loses its power. As I said earlier, it is best to think about what you want only when it pops into your head. In the beginning it is going to be on your mind all the time, but after a while you are not going to dwell on it as much. The rest of the time just focus on the present.

Do not try to change a bad outcome, replace a bad outcome. This is very important. Do not try to mentally undo what has happened by overanalyzing it. If something happens that you don't like, replace it with a different outcome.

Always focus first on the end result or goal, not the process by which you're going to get there. This is key.

As I said earlier, initially you may "feel like a bum" when you give up control of the outcome. You will feel defeated, but you are not defeated. It is your conscious mind that is defeated. That means you are doing it right. You have to let your subconscious mind make sense of your desires. Then it will rearrange the dream, and fulfill your goals. Let your subconscious mind handle it, it knows infinitely more than you do. You have to give up the desire to do it yourself.

Exercising and taking good care of yourself physically, is an excellent way to stay in the present moment. When you feel good in your body, it is far easier to stay present and enjoy it. If you are out of shape, and disgusted with your body, you will be more inclined to escape your reality by daydreaming about something better in the past or the future.

Don't try to rush the outcome. Let the outcome come to you. The Universe knows the perfect timing. There will usually be some lag time with your wishes, so slow down, have patience, and don't get ahead of yourself. To help you stay in the present, you also need to do little projects that give you instant gratification. These projects have to be something that allows you to build progress over time. Such as exercising or working on some kind of hobby.

Keep a tight schedule and do not procrastinate. Sticking to a schedule helps keep you in the present. Specify allotted times for everything you do, and once the time is up move on to the next thing. Keep your focus on conquering the next task. You need to discipline your day the same way you need to discipline your mind.

The more you focus on the present, the more powerful you become. As you look at everything in the present, you are building your empire. For every minute you focus on the present, you are ten times closer to achieving your goals. And, that's without putting in any extra effort. Think of it this way, imagine your goal as an arrow and you need to hit your target. Most people just grab the arrow and run as fast as they can to then place it on its intended target. Meanwhile you, first take some time to pull back on the arrow using a bow and then just let it go. You can shoot the arrow faster than you can running with it and at a greater distance with less effort.

If you are a student of metaphysics, you are familiar with the concept of gratitude. Gratitude works because it encourages you to appreciate your present reality. If you are grateful for the things you have right now, you don't need to go anywhere else for satisfaction. When you experience gratitude, your emotions are positive and it is easy to stay in the present.

By reading this book, you have already solved the biggest problems of your life. You know how to manifest things, so focus on the little problems, like staying in the present. All of your concerns about money, love, jobs, etc. are over. The only problem you have left is staying in the present. That is all there is.

Receiving is as important as asking. You receive by letting go, by not trying to control the outcome.

In order to create a heavy thought, one that will sink deep into your subconscious, you have to experience it. This is also key. When you think about what you want, take it beyond a thought to a full experience. It does not matter if it is perfect the first time, just keep rehearsing it in your head.

"I have the power to alter anything I see." Remember you are a God and this is just a dream, your dream. There is no reason to worry.

Have you ever had Deja Vu? When you do something new, but it feels like you have done it before? Usually it is an experience that you dreamed about a long time ago. Most people think they saw the future in their dream, but actually the reverse is true. The thought of the experience was in your subconscious and finally it happened in your waking dream (your life). In other words, you didn't have a dream about the future, you created the future!

You get everything in the order you ask. You **<u>always</u>** get everything in the order you asked. So, if you think about something that you want, and then afterwards you worry too much or think something negative, that negative thought will manifest itself after you get what you want. No exceptions.

There is no such thing as evil, good and evil are two sides of the same coin, which is reality. In other words you have to be stoic; you can't worry and become attached to stuff that happens to you whether good or bad.

Disciplining your mind is imperative. Practice the exercise I mentioned earlier. Pick an object you have in your home and focus on that object for at least five minutes a day. You will notice over time that you can focus longer and longer without other thoughts interfering.

Need vs. want. Sometimes wanting something is not enough. Feeling you need it, must have it, can't live without it, is a far stronger level of emotion. If you really want to manifest it, put yourself in a position of needing it. Think of your goal as something you must accomplish in this life. Feel like there is no way around it. This can be the level of feeling it takes to manifest some things.

# FREQUENTLY ASKED QUESTIONS

I'm usually asked what my view on God and religion is. Some years back a great teacher of mine introduced me to his concept of God and it's stuck with me ever since.

When god first created the Universe it was perfect, everything ran like clockwork. The planets behaved the way they were supposed to and so did Man and the animals, they didn't violate the laws of nature. God created something out of nothing, that's the first reality.

After some time God decided to create a second reality, in other words free will. So he created Lucifer, the smartest most powerful angel he ever created. Knowing that Lucifer would betray him. Lucifer decided to introduce the ability to reconfigure something that God already created into something new: i.e. technology and intellect. In other words not just take all the resources and minerals to alter the world around you, but also for Man to use his intellect to put together more choices on how to live his life. With this new ability Man now had the option to choose to live life God's way which is going with the flow of emotion and intuition or, use his ego to take charge and create his own destiny.

## HOW TO BECOME A GOD FOR BEGINNERS

Now it's Man's turn. God is waiting for Man to create a third reality. Man has both metaphysics along with intellect/ego as tools to bring about a new age for humanity. Will you be part of that change?

Some of my readers seem to be having problems with an important concept in my book and I wish to make a correction plus add this special page. It seems the readers are putting too much value on their specific goals and thereby having a hard time letting go. Also some people are easily manifesting the little things but are having a hard time manifesting the big things. I have changed the frequency of how many times you should remember your goals. Instead of morning and night, just focus on your thought whenever it pops into your mind and make sure it stays consistent. Don't let it change into something different. After a while it will pop up in your mind less often. Also, I will include this new page with a copy of my conversation with one of my readers explaining the rest of the changes. - Roberto Benitez

*Thank-you Roberto,*

*I can relate to what you say in you book that we have to bury our desires for manifestation and that's probably works because it will eliminate attachment. However at the same time, you say that we do need to think about what we want in the morning and in the night. I think if you really want something, you cannot help thinking about it.*

*Further, if we need to think of what we want rather than what we do not want, and we are in a particular situation which we don't want, to offset this, we do have to think of what we want, whether its in the morning or night.*

*As I said in my first sentence I do relate to what you say because at times there were particular things I wanted, I only thought once and then even forgot about it and it turned up. However when one's life is hanging on a balance, once cannot not think about it, if you have a method, I would be very, very grateful if you can tell me about it.*

*I liked your sentence that we should not worry and if we think we are being bums, then we are in the right direction….wow that is really powerful statement and it's really true*

*Thank-you Roberto once again. Looking forward for your response*

*Warm Regards Josephine*

*Hello Josephine,*

*And thank you for taking the time to write to me. I completely understand what you're trying to say. When you talk about your "life being in the balance" and it being hard to stay in the present and not constantly letting your mind wander to certain thoughts, that right there tells me that you're taking on too much responsibility! In the beginning I had the same problem and was trying to make one gigantic thought to solve all my problems, however it was so big it paralyzed me from doing anything else.*

*What you need to do is first take away the importance of that big goal. Don't think of it as a "big" goal anymore, just think of it as a "small desire" from now on. All your goals should really be small desires in your mind. Even if it's a brand new house you should only think of it as a "small desire", because you already know once you think about something that you're planning on getting, that's it! It eventually happens! That's why you were able to manifest little things you forgot about while the big things aren't happening. The goal is too big in your mind and you keep worrying about it. It should only just be just one of the many other simple desires you have.*

*For right now whatever big idea you have just know that's it's something that's coming your way soon. Don't think about it two times a day anymore, any time it comes up in your mind just make a mental note that's it's coming somehow some way. That should only take a couple of seconds. Think of your goal as something that you're going to have to deal with at some point. Like when you were a kid in high school. You have homework you don't want to do but at some point you have to deal with it. Same with your goal. Don't try to make it happen, just know that it's going to happen and you're going to have to deal with it at some point. But DON'T dwell on it. Think of your big goal as one of the many simple innocent desires you have. I know this paragraph sounds confusing but my main point is DO NOT force yourself to think about your "big" goal anymore, just be aware of your big goal as one of many desires that you already know is going to happen and you need to be ready for. That's it! No more effort. Focus on other things.*

*Once you start seeing a pattern of those thoughts manifesting themselves it will become second-nature and you will start to get more comfortable with this whole process and ready for bigger things. After a while of experiencing these "little successes" you're going to get to a point where you're not going to doubt that this stuff really works.*

*I'll give you a quick easy example. Many years ago I started a new job working for the government. I applied for this job two years before! It was an awesome job, good pay and it was a union job so the benefits were awesome. It took two years for it to happen because I didn't make any plans in my life until I got this job. In other words I put too much importance on this job so it never really got a chance to sink into my subconscious mind. Now mind you, before I applied for this job I thought about working for the government one morning and the very next day this job was posted in the newspaper. I took it as a sign and I applied. So what's the lesson? When I first had a simple innocent desire for the job it happened the very next day, once I stopped living my life waiting for them to call me back for the job it took two years!!! I put too much importance on the thought and that's not good, that's why it took so long! Another example: Using metaphysics I wanted to transfer out of my department to a better location just by having the intention to transfer in the back of my mind. A week later I found out about openings at a better location at my job for which I was approved! However my manager told me that they were holding me in my old position for six months because they were short staffed as it is. This time I didn't worry. I knew what my desire was so I didn't worry about it because I understand now that just having the desire is enough, I didn't need to put any more effort to get that transfer. I just kept on going about my daily business as if it was just another day. Eventually I was given the go-ahead for the transfer! This might sound stupid but it really is that simple. And like I said in my book. If you want to speed things up, STAY IN THE PRESENT MOMENT!!! I hope this helps, if you have more questions PLEASE don't hesitate to ask!*

*--Roberto*

# ABOUT THE AUTHOR

Having left his native Puerto Rico at the age of six Roberto, along with his mother and brother, were permanently transplanted to Boston, Massachusetts in 1985. Showing a passion for history at a young age, Roberto's early interests included politics and a passion for dissecting the mysteries of life. His interest in metaphysics began soon after meeting author Robert Kiyosaki in Phoenix, Arizona in 2006. He then joined the Invincible America course in Fairfield, Iowa; a private foundation made up of 2,500 meditators, with the purpose of creating a harmonizing and peaceful influence in the collective world consciousness through meditation. In 2008 he moved back to Boston, Massachusetts where he currently resides.

www.ingramcontent.com/pod-product-compliance
Lightning Source LLC
Chambersburg PA
CBHW071408040426
42444CB00009B/2153